Baby Animals
KANGAROOS

Kate Petty

Stargazer Books

Babies in pouches

Kangaroos belong to a group of animals called marsupials. Marsupial mothers carry their babies in a pouch. After only five weeks inside the mother's womb the baby kangaroo emerges, one twenty-thousandth of its mother's size.

   The baby is just one inch (2.5 cm) long and looks like a tiny bug. Using its "arms" it hauls itself up through its mother's fur to her pouch.

The baby crawls a distance of 6 inches (15 cm) to the pouch.

At this stage a marsupial baby is called a neonate. ▶

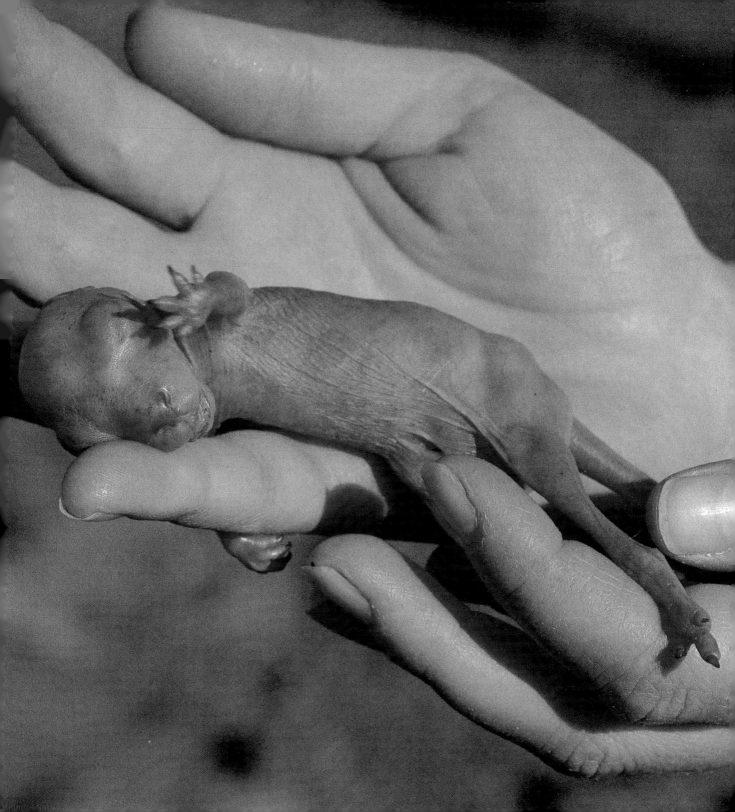

Inside the pouch

Inside the mother's pouch, the tiny kangaroo latches onto one of her four teats. The long teat swells to fill the baby's mouth, which stops it falling off while the mother hops about.

The baby stays in the pouch, drinking milk and growing very quickly. By the time it is two months old the baby is about the size of a domestic cat.

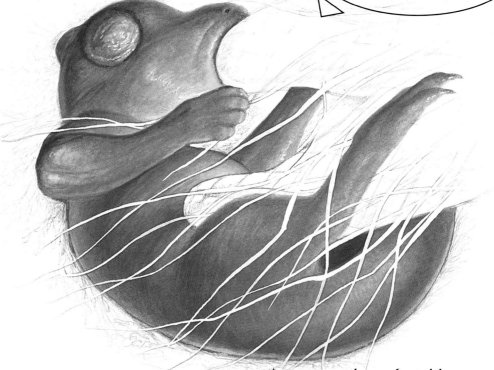

A neonate attached to one of its mother's teats

A warm and comfortable way to travel ▶

Joey

At about four months old the baby kangaroo begins to look like its parents, with a furry body, a black nose, and large dark eyes. Now it is known as a joey.

At about five months old the joey ventures outside of the pouch for the first time.

A very young joey

A young joey takes a look around. ▶

Time to explore

During the next few weeks the joey grows more adventurous and spends more and more time out of the pouch. At the first sign of danger, however, it dives straight back in, often head first, leaving its legs and tail hanging out.

The jocy must learn to hop about, feed itself, and keep clean. At just over seven months the joey leaves the pouch for the last time.

At first the young joey stays close to its mother.

The joey often returns to the safety of its mother's pouch. ▶

Feeding

The joey spends a lot of time grazing with other kangaroos and searching for water to drink. It also continues to suckle from one of its mother's teats.

By this time the mother has a new baby that has crawled up onto another of her teats. The mother is able to produce milk of different strengths to suit each of her babies.

This eight-month-old joey still drinks milk from its mother.

This joey has a choice of plants to nibble on. ▶

The kangaroo mob

A young kangaroo stays with its mother for about 20 months. They are part of a small group of kangaroos called a mob. An adult male, several females, and their joeys make up the mob.

Kangaroos move around in larger groups when food is plentiful. Wild dogs, called dingoes, and humans are their only real enemies.

A mob of kangaroos being chased by dingoes

A mob of kangaroos grazing ▶

Boxing and wrestling

Joeys play at boxing and wrestling. They will need to be able to defend themselves when they grow up. Adult male kangaroos fight one another to win females, too.

The young male kangaroos stalk about and scratch at themselves. They then wrestle with their forearms locked together and try to push each other over by kicking out with their feet.

Young males prepare for a mock battle.

Joeys boxing with each other ▶

Hopping along

The baby kangaroo's legs are a bit wobbly at first, but it soon learns to jump about on two legs. It pushes off with its long hind feet and uses its tail to balance.

Kangaroos hop along three feet (one meter) at a time but they can cover 26 feet (8 meters) in one leap when traveling fast. They can reach speeds of up to 40 mph (74 k/h).

The kangaroo's back legs are fantastically powerful.

Kangaroos on the move ▶

Growing up

Kangaroos live for about 15 years and continue to grow throughout their life. Females start having babies from about 18 months old and males are ready to mate from age three and a half. Female kangaroos only reach half the weight of the males.

The red kangaroo is the largest marsupial, standing taller than a man. Eastern Gray kangaroos are slightly smaller.

An Eastern Gray kangaroo

A Red kangaroo ▶

Wallabies

There are over forty different species of kangaroos. The smaller ones are called wallabies. They are native only to Australia but you can see them in zoos and wildlife reserves around the world.

A colony of red-necked wallabies lives wild in the north of England. They are descended from a pair that escaped from a private menagerie fifty years ago.

A Rock wallaby

A Bennett's wallaby ▶

Kangaroo facts

Kangaroos live in Australia. Kangaroos are quite hairless for the first three months but their hair has grown by the time they emerge from the pouch at five months.

   The baby is not completely weaned until it is about one year old, which is also when it molts for the first time. Kangaroos become independent from about two years.

Newborn

Index

© Aladdin Books Ltd 2006

*New edition published in the
United States in 2006 by:*
Stargazer Books
c/o The Creative Company
123 South Broad Street
P.O. Box 227
Mankato, Minnesota 56002

Designer: Pete Bennett – PBD
Editor: Rebecca Pash
Illustrator: George Thompson
Picture Research: Cee Weston-Baker

Printed in Malaysia
All rights reserved

Photographic credits:

Cover: PBD; pages 3, 15 and 17: Jen and Des Barlett / Bruce
Coleman; pages 5 and 19: John Cancalosi / Bruce Coleman; page
Fritz Prenzel / Bruce Coleman; page 9: Alan Root / Survival Anglia;
page 11: Jan Taylor / Bruce Coleman; page 13: Hans Reinhard / Br
Coleman; page 21: John Fawcett / Planet Earth.

Library of Congress Cataloging-in-Publication Data

Petty, Kate.
    Kangaroos / by Kate Petty.
       p. cm. -- (Baby animals)
    Includes index.
    ISBN 1-59604-036-X
       1. Kangaroos--Infancy--Juvenile literature. I. Title.

QL737.M35P48 2005
599.2'22139--dc22

                                    2004061468